AF593652

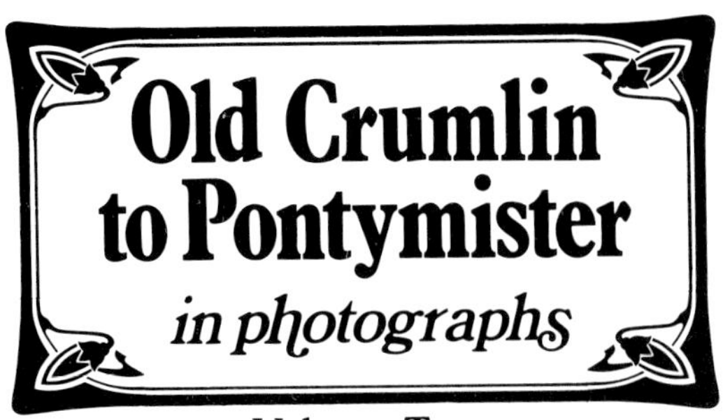

Volume Two

1 (*Overleaf*) The later stages of the demolition of Long Bridge, Risca, *c.*1900. Its 33 arches had been reduced to just four. The stones were used in the construction of Bridge Street

THE SIGNAL
ANSWERS
ANSWERS

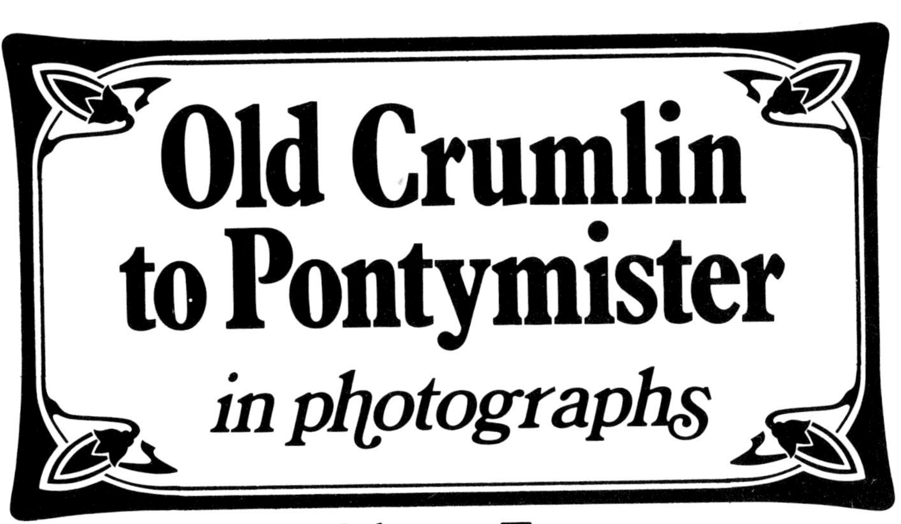

Old Crumlin to Pontymister in photographs

Volume Two

By Brian Collins and Terry Powell

FOREWORD
by
His Worship The Mayor
of the Borough of Islwyn
Councillor J. H. A. Roberts

STEWART WILLIAMS, PUBLISHERS

BARRY

First published in October, 1982

ISBN 0 900807 53 9

ACKNOWLEDGEMENTS

The authors' sincere thanks are extended to the following for allowing them to reproduce photographs from their collections:

Mrs E. A. Baber (218); R. Badge (74, 92, 119); Miss M. A. Barclay (212); T. Bartlett (198); D. Beavis (35, 104); J. Beavis (134, 168, 192); Mrs I. Beecham (21); Miss D. Benham (67, 193); Mrs M. T. Benjamin (202); Mrs M. Brown (130); B. J. Cawsey (150); Mrs L. A. Collins (80, 81); Mrs G. Croker (18); J. Davies (47, 49); Mrs M. Davies (203); Mrs N. Davies (42, 179); T. M. Davies (14, 145, 146, 174); L. Durban (36, 63, 84, 86, 163, 169); T. Edwards (61); W. Emmitt (44, 110); Mrs E. Evans (51, 172); Mrs D. Ford (187); A. E. Fryer (182); Miss D. George (50); Mrs M. George (115, 171); I. Greenslade (55); S. Griffin (160); H. Griffiths (31, 32, 96, 98, 127); Gwent Constabulary (208, 209, 219); Mrs M. Harris (85, 166, 167); J. L. Hatfield (25, 30, 125, 155, 156); L. Hawkins (113, 114); Mrs E. Hicks (165); N. Hicks (12, 149); Mrs S. E. Hillier (73, 76, 97, 210); Mrs P. Hockey (1, 102, 136, 138); Miss O. Holley (46, 147); E. Hopkins (38, 112); O. Hopkins (116, 173, 175); W. Hughes (204); H. O. Humphreys (58); J. Hyde (52); Mrs M. James (16, 17, 91, 118); Mrs G. Jandrell (99); L. Jenkins (39, 40); Mrs P. Jennings (56); P. Jennings (22, 28, 29); W. G. John (68); Mrs A. C. Jones (159); B. J. Jones (54, 59, 62); N. D. Jones (82, 153, 214); R. Jones (94, 206); W. Jones (200); Knight Bros. (3, 20, 24, 95); Mrs D. Knight (27, 181); F. Lane (180); Mrs E. Maddocks (66, 100, 132, 186, 189, 190, 215); Mrs M. Marsh (45); T. Marsh (7, 15, 111); Mrs O. Miles (6, 105, 106); B. S. Milsom (133); G. E. Morgan (10, 23); G. I. Morgan (101, 183, 184); Mrs J. Morgan (129); W. Morris (34); W. J. Morse (151); Mrs J. Palmer (139); Mrs G. Parfitt (121, 122); P. Parry (2); P. Peacock (143); G. Phelps (176); Mrs I. Phillips (157); Miss A. Pinnell (120); Mrs E. J. Powell (188); Mrs P. Powell (109); Mrs W. M. Powell (194); Mrs I. Price (158); Mrs L. Pritchard (41, 107, 170); Mrs D. Prosser (8, 144, 201); B. Protheroe (211); Mrs J. Ralph (93); Mrs G. Richards (195, 199); I. G. Roberts (217); Mrs M. A. Roberts (178); J. C. Rodway (103, 177, 191); Miss Z. Rogers (26); R. Saunders (72); J. S. Selby (19, 205); J. Shepherd (87); Mrs V. Simmonds (117); Mrs A. V. Stephens (69, 90); V. Stock (148, 164); Mrs F. M. Stokes (88, 89); Mrs C. Thomas (216); Mrs G. Thomas (43); M. Thomas (135, 140); Mrs N. Thomas (60, 71, 75, 79, 154); Mrs P. Thomas (83, 128, 161, 162); R. J. Thomas (123, 124, 152, 207); Mrs G. Tiley (64); Mrs C. Tooze (126); Mrs L. Vincent (5, 70, 141); Mrs I. Ward (57, 65, 77, 78, 213); P. H. Wayman (131); D. Weare (13); Mrs M. Westlake (185); Mrs N. Williams (137); T. J. Woodford (196); R. Woodford (108, 142, 197); Mrs D. M. Wrighton (53). Other photographs are from the authors' own collections.

Printed in Wales by D. Brown & Sons Ltd., Cowbridge and Bridgend, Glamorgan

Foreword

by His Worship The Mayor of the Borough of Islwyn, Councillor J. H. A. Roberts

For many years, in company with many others, I travelled the tortuous route from Pontymister to Crumlin. My journey started at the crossing where trains frequently interrupted the traffic flow to rattle across to the steelworks. It continued along the always crowded Risca streets to negotiate the bridge at Crosskeys corner, the awkward Pontywaun bridges and factory trip. Leaving Cwmcarn, we often had to wait to allow a down coming 'bus to pass before entering Abercarn. We then proceeded either left past the tin works site of the West End and along the precarious road above the Celynen Colliery, or kept right past the Ranks and Chapel of Ease through a deep valley between shale tips and mountain to turn left to Newbridge Railway Station; then on to the School of Mines at Crumlin—the view dominated by the majestic viaduct. The road crossed and recrossed the railway line with its nose to tail trucks of coal making for the coast and the canal where my great grandfather once plied his barge.

How the scene has changed! Many of the landmarks mentioned have disappeared, some almost imperceptibly, others dramatically as when the canal from Pontywaun to Crumlin became a by-pass road. Cinemas have come and gone and shops such as Wallace Jones, which served the community for generations and boasted Newbridge, Abercarn and Risca on its boards, have made way for others.

How great were the changes when canal, railway, mines and works came to the Ebbw Valley and great they were when they were replaced. And so it continues with the by-pass of Risca, the by-pass out of Crumlin and the proposed new road from Newbridge through Pentwynmawr to Blackwood. This second volume gives us a view of those who brought about, and those who endured, the changes.

Photographs have, once again, made the past present and brought the distant near. Some have called up our predecessors before us with their peculiarities of dress; they have admitted us to their work, their worship, their play and their leisure. Others have unlocked our frozen memories, as we recognise relatives and friends and acquaintances of youth. This book is a tribute to those who 'along the cool sequestered vale of life kept the noiseless tenor of their way'. They gave life to the valley and to us.

We are indebted again to Dr Collins and Mr Powell for another excellently presented book of photographs and I am privileged in offering a foreword.

J. H. A. Roberts

Introduction

Publication of the first volume of old photographs of the lower part of the Western Valley of Gwent made many people, both residents and those who may have moved away, realise that they too had material which in some way helped to record the past. The area with which we are again concerned includes the townships of Crumlin, Newbridge, Pentwynmawr, Abercarn, Cwmcarn, Pontywaun, Crosskeys, Risca and Pontymister.

The books are not intended to provide a history, but careful study of the photographs will remind more mature readers of the good and the bad times. Younger people, who may perhaps take modern aids and facilities for granted, are encouraged to reflect upon the achievements of the past, not least in this neighbourhood, which were brought about by great ingenuity and dedication from all sectors of the community.

Based in the main upon coal mining and iron making, early residential and commercial development may not be well suited to modern living or to motor transport. However, so many houses and other buildings, often over a hundred years old, were so solidly constructed that they remain and are readily identified in the very old views. This will accentuate the nostalgia felt in browsing through the pages.

Evidence of early transport systems also remains, with the lower reaches of the Crumlin Branch of the Monmouthshire Canal intact below Pontywaun. The Sirhowy and Halls Tramroads were converted into and supplemented by more updated railways, which in turn have been restricted by more recent economic measures. The inflexibility of the railways, even at their peak, led to the development and expansion of 'bus routes and services. Yet again these have been severely affected by increasing car ownership.

Many of the trades and industries of the past appear to be far more interesting, and perhaps more romantic, than their present-day counterparts. However, it is only too easy to forget the sweat and the toil associated with the former. Supermarkets and chain stores have greatly affected smaller village shops—especially the traditional 'corner shops'—with further aggravation being inflicted through the construction of by-pass roads which draw away potential passing trade.

In sport, the valley has produced its champions and its many experts, but more importantly, many thousands of participants from all walks of life. Rugby, soccer and cricket clubs have existed in the individual townships for many years, but so many other teams from streets, works, offices, etc., have offered wide opportunities for keen competition. Other popular outdoor activities have included bowls, tennis and cycling, whilst indoors, boxing, billiards, snooker, gymnastics, table tennis, darts and others have contributed to the welfare of the resident population.

Being a traditional Welsh industrial valley, the inhabitants have proved to be well capable of entertaining themselves and others around them. Large numbers of choral societies, glee societies, male-voice parties and concert parties have existed, and several still perform. Plays and operettas were at one time regularly produced at the different churches and chapels, where, unlike today, such regular meeting together by so many people, either for religious or social purposes, contributed very much to the formation of a strong community spirit.

Out of this community spirit has come the inspiration and desire to devote large parts of lives to public service. There has not been a shortage of such 'martyrs' working for public bodies and charities for the good of the district and of its people. In times of strife and of war, so many have served with honour, some making the extreme sacrifice. Tragedies in other spheres of life have included colliery disasters, floods, and the air crash at Llandow in 1950 which affected the whole area in one way or another.

These are some of the aspects of the past which are captured in the following pages. It is hoped that they will bring back as many memories and stir up as much comment as those in the first collection. An apology is given for including in volume one a photograph of Celynen North Colliery instead of Blackvein Colliery as intended. This is now rectified within.

The authors wish to thank again all the contributors who have supplied photographs, information, advice and encouragement, together with the senders of the many kind letters received following the publication of the first book. Further thanks are due to His Worship the Mayor of the Borough of Islwyn, Councillor J. H. A. Roberts, for so readily agreeing to write the Foreword, and to the Publisher, Stewart Williams, for making the whole thing possible, and for adding this part of Gwent to his excellent series of photographic histories.

Brian Collins Terry Powell

The Townships

2 Crumlin, *c.*1900, showing the level crossing in the Square, and the Hall looking like a castle amidst the trees

3 An earlier view more to the north with the Trinant road merely a track, and Pritchard's brewery the large building lower right

4 Disaster in Commercial Road, Crumlin. On 18 June 1915 all four stores were gutted by fire. They were later converted into houses, with the pillars shown in the photograph still evident

5 Crumlin Square, *c.*1912. The Cyclists' Rest was on the site of the present Workmen's Institute

6 Main Street, Crumlin, *c.*1900, showing the houses (behind the gas-lamp) which were demolished to give access to the station when the new road bridge was built

7 Main Street again, *c.*1900

8 Mr & Mrs William Mustoe with their grand-daughter Esther, outside Bush Cottage, Treowen, 1890

9 A view from the old tramroad behind Beynon Street, Newbridge, before Celynen North Colliery was sunk. Bush Cottage can just be made out top left

10 Newbridge Police Station to the left, and a shopping complex in the building now housing the Labour Club, *c.*1910

11 *Newbridge Hotel* and Square before the roads were made up, *c.*1905

12 High Street, Newbridge, *c.*1905. The building to the right of the picture is now part of the Co-operative Society stores

13 Further up the High Street, Newbridge Institute photographed *c.*1910

14 A view over Tynewydd School, *c.*1905. Constuction of the houses in the foreground are nearing completion, and a farm is seen on the site of the present Vicarage

15 Turning the camera a little to the right, it is seen that Windsor Avenue and the upper end of Tynewydd Terrace have yet to be built

16/17 Two views of High Street, Pentwynmawr, *c.*1910

Chapel of Ease, Abercarn

18 Looking towards Chapel of Ease from the West End, with the barns of Abercarn House seen in the foreground

19 Roadworks, 1920s fashion, at Chapel of Ease!

LOVERS LANE, ABERCARN.

20 A general view of Abercarn from the west, *c.*1900, with Lady Llanover's Welsh Church seen on the hill

21 Another view of Abercarn from the south, with the Colliery's No. 1 Pit in the foreground

22 West End, Abercarn, *c.*1905, with the old iron foundry just showing above the trees to the left. The gasworks were transferred to the other side of the river in the early fifties

23 Islwyn Street, Abercarn, *c.*1905. The entrance to the old Vicarage is seen near the lamp post

24 High Street, Abercarn, *c.*1920

25 A distinctly military flavour to the Church Parade passing along High Street, Abercarn, in 1913

26 An oil painting by local artist Kem Rogers, of Chapel Farm, Cwmcarn, as it appeared in 1915. The farm was built near the site of an old monastery chapel and is now occupied by the Comprehensive School. Nearby Chapel Farm Terrace was nicknamed Skeleton Row after excavation for the foundations unearthed human remains

27 Reflections of Brierly Place from the old canal bridge at Cwmcarn. The canal was filled to make way for the by-pass road

28/29 Two views along Newport Road, Cwmcarn, in 1913

30 Newport Road, Cwmcarn, in 1950, with Postmaster Garnet Humphries in the right foreground

31 A very old picture of Factory Trip, Pontywaun, with Twyncarn House, now a day-nursery, commanding the landscape

Factory Trip, Cwmcarn

32 A later view of Factory Trip, illustrating the development and the growth of vegetation by 1920

33 St Mary's Church, Risca, taken before the Sunday School was built on the field in the foreground in 1891

34 A view of Risca, before the turn of the century, taken from the old copper works towards Fernlea. Many buildings seen have been replaced, and the quarry has noticeably eaten into the hillside

35 A later view of Risca and Pontymister taken from Ocherwyth

36 The Old Colliery Bridge, Risca, damaged by flooding in 1930. Colliery Place can be seen in the background

37 A much more open aspect for Gelli Crescent in the 1930s

Gelli Crescent – Risca

Sports and Entertainments

38/39/40 Three of the many boxers from the area who have delighted the whole of Wales. Edgar Evans and Selwyn Evans, Professional Champions of Wales, and Parry Dando, Welsh ABA Champion

41 Viaduct Terrace street cricket team welcome back George Coleman (*centre front*) after receiving his medal for bravery underground

42 Crumlin Workingmen's Club and Institute Skittles Team, 1938, winners of the B Section Cup from 1934 to 1938

43 Crumlin High level Schools' Rugby Team, 1919/20, champions of the Abercarn and District Schools' Rugby League, and holders of the Ivy Cup, seen here with Headmaster Walter Jones. Played 33, won 33, points for 793, points against 21

44 Crumlin Rugby XV, 1924/25, with captain Jim Jones

45 Constitutional Club, Newbridge, Skittles Team, *c.*1910

46 One of the many successful Newbridge Bowls Teams pose with their President, Miss Elsie Price, who held that somewhat unusual post from 1927 to 1946

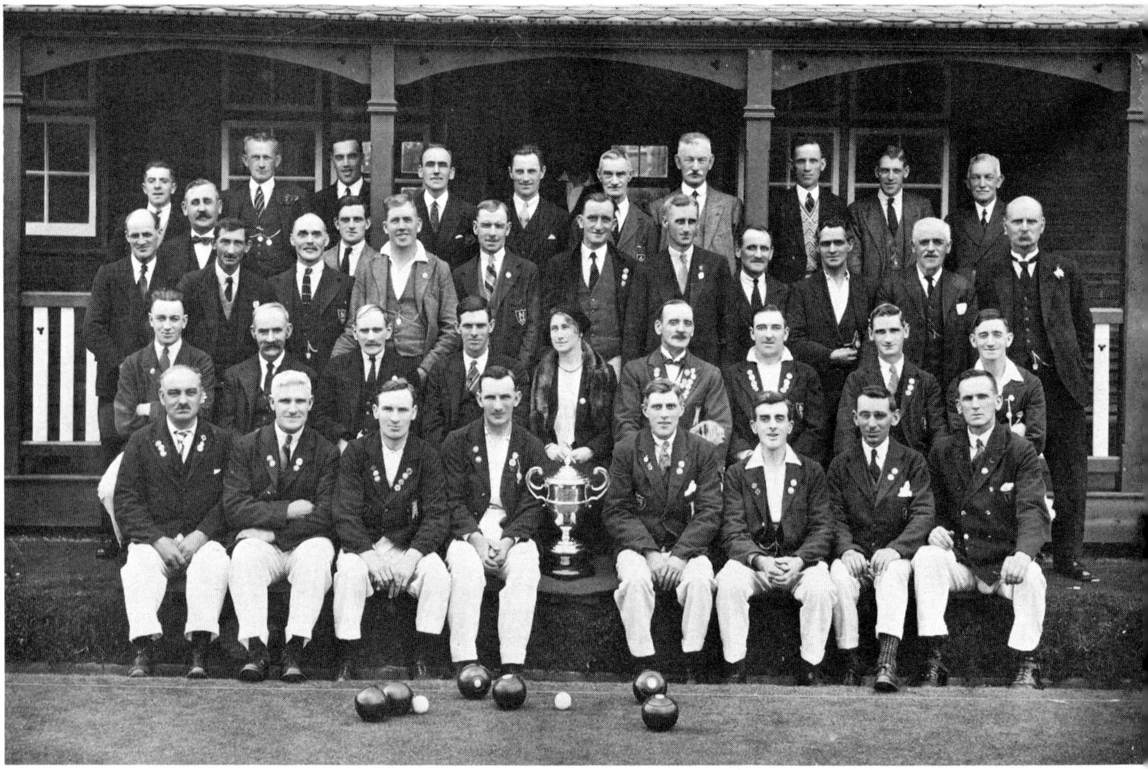

47 Newbridge RFC, Monmouthshire Rugby League Champions 1926, with captain Wyndham Price

48 Newbridge Rugby Team, 1942/43, with captain Norman Harris

49 Newbridge Boys' Club Gymnastic Display Team, with leader Walter O'Connor, 1951

50 Bryngwyn AFC, Newbridge, 1933/34, with leader Arthur Hall

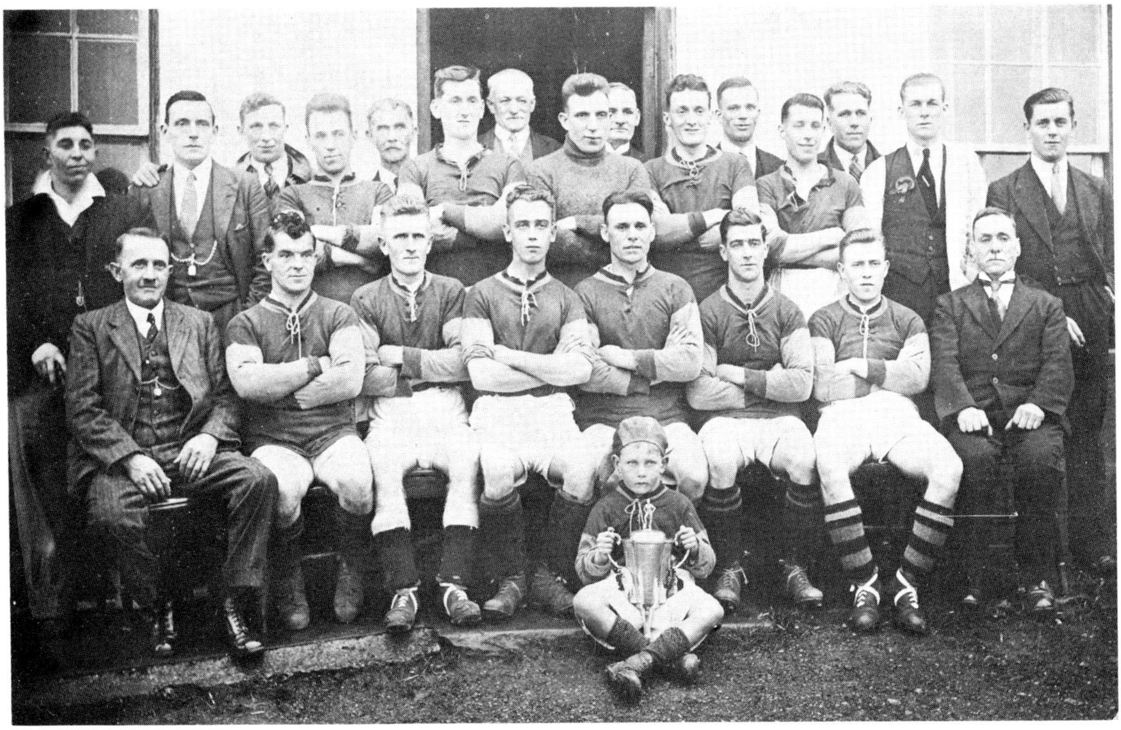

51 Pentwynmawr Soccer Team, 1929, winners of the Abertillery and District League Cup

52 Abercarn Tinplaters Memorial Institute Billiard Teams, 1933/34, who enjoyed notable success in the Western Valley League

53 Abercarn Rugby Team, with captain T. Eatwell, winners of the Ben Francis Cup in the 1935/36 season

54 Roy Burnett, from Abercarn, throws his boots into the River Usk in 1958, to mark the end of a long and distinguished rugby career which brought him international honours and much popularity

55 Abercarn Reserves, 1920/21

56 Abercarn Stars, 1925

57 Abercarn Bowling Club members in the early 1960s. The club was formed in 1920

58 A cycle race at the Welfare Ground, Abercarn, *c.*1950. Leading the field is Ted Harrhy of Cwmcarn Paragons, holder of many South Wales Track Championships

59 Cwmcarn-born Welsh rugby internationals, Jack Hurrell, Des Greenslade and Brian Jones, seen here in the Newport strip in 1963/64

60 Cwmcarn Youth Club Leader, Mrs Nel Thomas, with the Hockey Team, *c.*1942

61 Crosskeys Cricket XI, *c.*1930

62 Crosskeys Rugby Team, which included a number of international players, holders of the Unofficial Welsh Championship in 1935/36. The captain was W. Ward

63 Risca Harlequins, 1936, winners of the W. J. Wall Cup and the Newport & District Cup, with captain Harry Tucker. In the centre of the group is Dan Jones, President of the Monmouthshire Union and a member of the 'Big Five'

64 Risca Park Stars AFC, winners of the 1st Division Newport and District League, 1920/21, with captain T. Eaton

65 Pontywaun County School Rugby Team, 1929/30

66 Pontywaun County School Hockey Team, 1927

67 Pontymister Athletic Juniors, *c.*1920, with captain G. Bushel

68 Risca and Dan-y-Graig Schools combined rugby team, 1947/48

69 'David the Shepherd Boy' performed by Bethel Baptist Church, Crumlin, in 1919

70 Crumlin Workingmen's Club and Institute Glee Society, with conductor E. Jenkins, winners at Crumlin Eisteddfod in 1917. Both the above photographs were taken in the grounds of Crumlin Hall

71 Crumlin High Level School Sword Dancers, *c.*1927. The team was trained by Miss Blodwen Hume

72 The Excelsior Glee Singers of Newbridge, photographed in 1928, with conductor Gethin Hopkins, accompanist Miss Ceinwen Hopkins and elocutionist Miss Molly Abbott

73 The cast of 'A Midsummer Night's Dream' at Newbridge Secondary School, *c.* 1938

74 Abercarn Welsh Church Dramatic Society's production of 'A Hundred Years Old' at the Memorial Hall, Newbridge, 1939

75 Abercarn Playgoers Society production of 'The Idol', written by Gil Thomas (*seated centre*) *c.*1928

76 Abercarn Silver Prize Band, *c.*1945, with bandleader Tom Morgan

77 Mrs Schneider crowns Carnival Queen Miss Dorothy Bullock at the Council Offices, Abercarn, *c.*1950. Also in the picture are George Moses, Ivor Collins and Frank Edwards

78 Carnival barrel organ at Cwmcarn in the 1950s, with Ike Greenslade, Mervyn Hyde, George Browning, Graham Barnes and Charlie Franklyn

79 Cwmcarn Youth Club's presentation of 'Princess Ju Ju' in 1949

80 Cwmcarn Relief Fund Choir whose concert tours made valuable contributions in aid of the strikers of 1926 and their dependents

81 The Dorian Singers photographed in the foyer of the Olympia Cinema, Cardiff, in 1947, when they sang at the premiere of the film 'The Corn is Green'

82 Pontywaun Gleemen, *c.*1953, photographed at Grosmont, near Abergavenny

83 Cast of 'A Village Fayre', performed at the Primitive Methodist Church, Crosskeys, *c.*1922

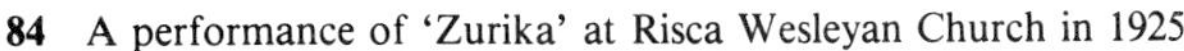

84 A performance of 'Zurika' at Risca Wesleyan Church in 1925

85 Oxford House Ladies' Community Group of 1943 with their production of 'Joan of Arc'

86 Oxford House Players, winners of the British Final at the One-Act Community Drama Festival held at Coventry in 1961

87 Risca Choral Society photographed in rural surroundings in Dan-y-Graig fields, 1926

Transport

88 The old and the 'new' Lewis and James Western Valley omnibuses outside *Railway Hotel*, Crumlin, 1926

89 At the same time, a taxi calls at Wall's hardware store. The shops with the awnings on the right were later destroyed by fire

90 Dr Ryan's family and nursemaid make an elegant picture in 1903

91 Pony and trap at Pentwynmawr, driven by young Tom Jones

92 Newton and Reg Badge display their new acquisition in Meredith Terrace, Newbridge, 1910

93 Will Stevens, with bicycle, also of Meredith Terrace, poses with another form of transport at Llanhilleth

94 A charabanc-load of Abercarn punters about to leave for the races in the twenties

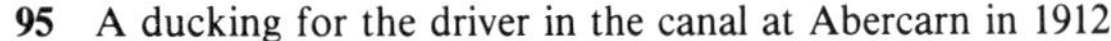

95 A ducking for the driver in the canal at Abercarn in 1912

96 Charlie Davies, proud owner of this Douglas motorcycle

97 Elsie Williams of Cwmcarn with her 'baby' in 1918

98 Thomas Griffiths, haulage contractor of Cwmcarn, seen here on a cable-laying expedition at Ystrad Mynach

99 Jesse Herbert of Risca, who was foreman at Cox's Quarry, Crosskeys, photographed around 1890

100 Clearly, Swansea was not too far to go from Crosskeys, *c.*1912!

101 Wedding cars supplied by J. B. Thomas Ltd., *c.*1937, with drivers Geoff Morgan and David Hughes

102 William Mogford at Church Road Terrace, Risca

103 Howell Pugh takes his class from Bethany Church for an outing to Talgarth in Philpot's charabanc in 1922

104 Straight from the makers—the latest addition to the Beavis fleet!

Trade and Industry

105 The long and dangerous task of painting Crumlin Viaduct. In October 1914 one of the painters, James Dally, was awarded a certificate of bravery for saving the life of a colleague after an accident in which another man died

106 Staff of Crumlin High Level Station in the nineteen twenties

107 Tom Howse in the fitting shop at Navigation Colliery in 1909. Mr Howse was one of the many men who completed over fifty years at the same colliery

108 Mrs E. A. Williams outside her shop in Crown Street, Crumlin, in the 1920s. Mrs Williams caught the 5 am train to Newport each day to pick up produce from the wholesale market

109 A typical 'house' shop. Samuel Porter and his wife Sarah at William Street, Crumlin, in 1915

110 Mr Wall with his helper Ross Maidment at their shop in Crumlin. The price on the shovels is 10½d!

111 Mr Jenkins at Hillside, Crumlin, *c.*1910

112 Tom Marsh, blacksmith, with an audience at his Cwmdows forge in 1928

113/114 The winding gear being installed at Celynen North Colliery, *c.* 1915

115 The original coaching inn of Newbridge, now demolished. It stood on the road which led from the *Beaufort Arms* to the Railway Station. The inn was used as a synagogue in the latter part of the nineteenth century

116 Mill Farm, which was situated at the lower end of Beynon Street, Newbridge. Its land was taken over by Celynen South Colliery

117 An illicit mineshaft behind Fields Park, Newbridge, in 1926

118 Tom Jones at his butcher's shop in High Street, Pentwynmawr

119 Staff of the many Jones and Porter stores in the area in 1927

120 Newbridge and Abercarn ambulance class for Great Western Railway employees, 1914/15

121/122 Two views of Prince of Wales Colliery, Abercarn, soon after the explosion of 1878 which claimed 264 lives. Note the engine named Gen. Williams, the flat-wheeled mine trams, and the haystack where Rhyswg Road was later built

123 William Mogford's store at Llanfach, Abercarn, with Jack Thomas, Mrs Ada Harris, Mrs Winifred Mogford, William Mogford, Mrs Florie Thomas and young Ron Thomas. The site is now occupied by R. J. Thomas' The Stores

124 Cold Rolls Department at Abercarn Tinworks, *c.* 1925

125 Griff Davies' outfitter's shop at Newport Road, Cwmcarn, in 1927, with Jack Hatfield, Jack Thomas and Fred Rees

126 No shortage of staff at Star Supply Stores, Newport Road, Cwmcarn, in 1926

127 Some of the 14 colts produced by the mare held by Mrs Edith Griffiths. Thomas Griffiths, haulage contractor, is on the left, and George Yearsley second from the right. The photograph was taken in 1905

128 Crosskeys Co-op Staff, *c.* 1923, with manager Alfred Williams (holding bowler)

129 Bill-poster by day and projectionist by night, Trevor Watts (*on the left*) advertises the latest thriller at the Variety Palace, Crosskeys, *c.*1912

130 'Little Jackie' in charge of the cart of Ambrose & Son, Confectioners, Crosskeys

131 Post Office staff at Crosskeys, 1913

132 One of the maintenance gangs at Risca Colliery which continued to work during the 1926 strike

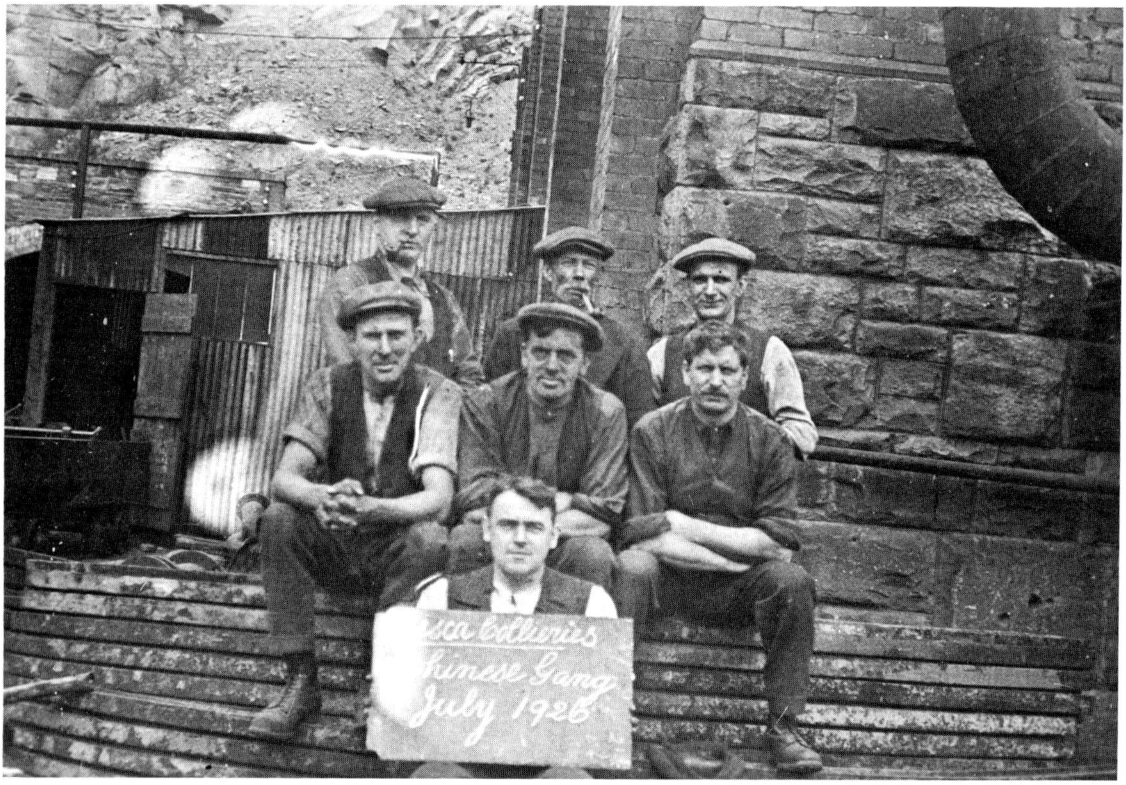

133 Blackvein Colliery photographed in about 1930

134 Workers at Dan-y-Graig Brickworks in 1937, with owner Mr Southward-Jones (wearing trilby hat)

135 Risca Post Office in 1907, with Miss Elsie Thomas, Mervil Thomas and postmaster James Thomas. The site is now occupied by Beavis' butcher's shop

136 Longstaff's Bazaar, Risca, *c.*1930, with manageress Miss Sarah Mogford on the right

137 Mrs Doris Hill of Pontymister wearing the ticket collector's uniform of the GWR in 1919

138 Risca station staff in the early forties

139 The lower end of Pontymister seen through the steelworks' stacks, *c.*1930

140 Steelworkers at Pontymister (*back row*): William Kyte, Ted Hemmings, Jimmy Thomas, Cliff Davies and Cliff Robins; (*front row*): Mervil Thomas, Eddie Maddocks and Wyndham Davies

Religion and Education

141 Deacons of Bethel Baptist Church, photographed in the grounds of Crumlin Hall in 1926

142 Bethel Annual Christmas Concert in 1930, with Minister Rev. Maddocks

143 The evangelist Evan Roberts on a visit to Newbridge in 1908

144 A group of workers for the St Paul's Church, Newbridge, Building Fund, in 1920, with Rev. D. Hopkins

145 Laying of foundations for Temple Church, Newbridge, in 1912. Demyl, the Church which it replaced, can be seen in the background

146 Rev. J. Vardre James takes to the open air below Pennar Street to gather support for the new church

147 Shortly after the renovation of Wesley Hall Church, Newbridge, *c.*1938

148 A Garden Party at the Wesleyan Church, *c.*1930

149 St Luke's Church Guild, Abercarn, photographed outside the old church, *c.*1920—later used as an office by Wallace Jones Ltd

150 Warrant Officer Bernard Cawsey leads the Church Lads' Brigade Band past Victoria Hall, Abercarn, *c.*1946. The Salvation Army Hall has now been converted into the Victoria Service Station

151 The Church in Abercarn built by Lady Llanover in an attempt to perpetuate the Welsh language. Services in Welsh continued until the late nineteen seventies

152 Sisterhood at Central Hall, Abercarn, *c.*1925

153 Deacons of the English Baptist Church, Abercarn, *c.*1930

154 Girls of Cwmcarn Youth Club, *c.*1946, with leader Mrs Nell Thomas, pictured outside the Church Hall

155 Choir at St John's Church, Cwmcarn, *c.*1923, with vicar Rev. J. W. James

156 A play called 'Jan of Windmill Land' enacted at St John's Church in 1923

157 Crosskeys Methodist Church Bible Class, 1902

158 Renovation of Hope Baptist Church, Crosskeys, during the 1898 strike

159 Adult Band of Hope workers at Hope Baptist Church in 1912

160 Mrs Osborne's Sunday School class at Hope, *c.*1950

161 Primitive Methodist Church Choir, Crosskeys, 1909, with conductor T. A. Sage

162 Laying of the foundation stone for the Primitive Methodist Church Hall, Crosskeys, in 1912, by Miss Hilda Rogers, later to become Mrs Sam Wynne

163 Children's Cantata at a picnic party held by the Risca Primitive Methodist Church Sunday School in 1913

164 Moriah Sunday School ladies group in the early nineteen thirties

165 At about the same time, the young people's group at Moriah Baptist Church, with the Rev. and Mrs Owen

166 The Methodist Chapel at Risca, built in 1846, which was damaged by flooding in 1891. The congregation met in neighbouring schools until the building was replaced in 1893

167 Early day officers of Pontymister Salvation Army display a fine variety of instruments

168 The Anniversary in 1956 of forty years of leadership of the Pontymister Salvation Army Songsters by William Hold

169 Risca Welsh Methodists' International Fellowship, 1931, with Rev. Leon Atkin

170 Standard III at Crown Street Junior School, Crumlin, 1919, with teacher Mr Protheroe

171 A very early photograph, *c.*1875, at Crumlin Infants' School, when even the animals went on parade!

172 Crumlin High Level, 1913, with a youthful Talbot Thomas, teacher, later to become Deputy Headmaster at Newbridge Grammar School (see 176)

173 St David's Day, 1917 style, at Tynewydd Junior School, Newbridge

174 The teacher in this Tynewydd class group, Albert Prout, served for over forty years at the school—from 1926 until his retirement in 1967

175 George William Stocker, the first Headmaster of Greenfield Boys' School, Newbridge, photographed in 1913

176 Newbridge Grammar School Cricket XI, *c.*1949, with Headmaster A. T. S. Cooke, Deputy Headmaster Talbot Thomas and Gamesmaster Idris Roberts

177 Standard IV Gwyddon School Abercarn 1928 with teacher L C Rodway

178 West End School, Abercarn. Collars were the order of the day for Standard I in 1910

179 The Art lesson is interrupted for a photograph at West End School in 1925

180 Standard I at Cwmcarn Junior School, 1923, with Headmaster Mr Sutton and teacher Miss Hurley

181 Staff at Cwmcarn School, 1934/35. (*Back row*): B. Charlottes, Miss M. Smithyman, W. Rawlings, Mrs N. Holland, G. Powell, Miss I. Hurley; (*Middle row*): A. Marsh, Miss N. Hale, Miss E. Davies, J. Coker, Headmaster, Miss K. Simpson, Miss W. Powell, H. Jones; (*Front*): Miss E. Saunders, Miss M. Roberts

182 Class I at Cwmcarn Infants' School in 1927

183 Crosskeys Infants' School, Class 3, 1926/27, with teacher Miss Kelsall and Headmistress Mrs Burton

184 A Crosskeys Infants' class in 1942

185 Well over 40 pupils in this Infants' class at Waunfawr in 1929

186 Things had obviously not changed from 1914, but at least we see here two monitors to offer help to the teacher

187 Standard 5 at Risca Junior School, *c.*1940, with teacher Miss Stevens

188 Learning shoe repairs at Oxford House, Risca, *c*.1931. The pupil on the left is Fred Powell

189 Form II, Pontywaun County School, 1922

190 A group of ex-Pontywaun County School pupils at University College of Wales, Aberystwyth, *c.*1930

191 Pontymister Boys' School, Standard III, 1913, with Headmaster E. Williams, and teacher Fred Jones

192 Pontymister Infants' in 1934. Surely one of the pupils prepared the notice!

193 Miss Mary Milton's class at Pontymister Infants' School in 1944

194 Pontymister Infants' again in 1938

Public Service and Special Events

195 General Booth, founder of The Salvation Army, arrives in Crumlin in 1906

196 Volunteers on parade outside The Temperance House in Crumlin Square, *c.*1913

197 The Founders of Crumlin Workingmen's Club and Institute, which was opened on 12 September 1914

198 Crowds turn out in Main Street, Crumlin, *c.*1910, to see a procession leaving The Hall

199 Tea up at the Whitsun Picnic in 1911 at Third's Field, Crumlin

200 Lt. Tom Maiden's platoon of the Home Guard outside the Constitutional Club, Newbridge, in the early nineteen forties

201 The Newbridge Bandage Class, organised by Mrs Gregg, during the First World War

202 Hardly a rival company, the Newbridge Red Cross Society pictured about the same time

203 Celynen North Colliery Ambulance Team, *c.*1925, display some of their trophies. The team, which included five Coleman brothers, is seen here with Colliery Manager Mr Evans

204 Charity Ball, held at the Memorial Hall, Newbridge, in the early nineteen thirties, in aid of the Royal Gwent Hospital. The organiser was Jack Morris (*front right*)

205 Flowers for the children, cauliflowers for the men—a strange gathering at Chapel of Ease in 1921

206 The opening of the Prince of Wales Industrial Estate, Abercarn. Prime Minister Harold Wilson meets Reg Jones and his goat Chocolate

207 The opening of the Fire Station at Abercarn on 12 March 1924, with the Fire Service represented by Captain Booth. A new station was built in 1976

208 Security Police checking supplies brought by Trevor Burgess, a Newport taxi proprietor, during the strike at Cwmcarn Colliery in 1921

209 Policemen set up a field kitchen at Cwmcarn Colliery during the 1921 strike. The strike contingent was made up from officers drafted from the Newport force

210 Cwmcarn Constitutional Old Men's Outing Club about to set off on their annual outing to Gloucester and Cheltenham on August Bank Holiday, 1924. The Chairman was H. J. Westwood (*fourth left, second row*)

211 Cwmcarn Auxiliary Fire Service, 1942/43

212 A line-up of Brownies at the Drill Hall, Cwmcarn, 1939. Chapel Farm can just be seen in the background

213 Men's Section at the British Legion, Cwmcarn, in the early nineteen fifties

214 St John Ambulance Brigade, Cwmcarn, 1940

215 Crosskeys Territorials of the Royal Field Artillery, *c.*1913

216 The Lord Mayor of Cardiff arrives at Risca in 1912 for the Bedwellty Show. The farmhouse in the background was on the site of the present Ty Isaf complex

217 A 'tank day' held at Risca in 1919 by the War Savings Association, Risca Urban District Council Local Central Committee, which raised £85,214

218 Risca Home Guards towards the end of the Second World War

219 Risca Division of the Monmouthshire Constabulary, 1925